SCIENCE

Not Just for Scientists!

EASY EXPLORATIONS FOR YOUNG CHILDREN

Leonisa Ardizzone, EdD

DEDICATION

for Rafaella

ACKNOWLEDGMENTS

I gratefully acknowledge the support and guidance of these people:

My parents, Ron and Marie, who made me the explorer I am; two exceptional science teachers, Ms. Bell and Ms. Eisner, who set me on my scientific path many moons ago;Ms. Lucille Schmeider and Dr. Mildred Brammer, former science professors who continue to believe in me; my numerous progressive education colleagues from twenty-plus years in the field; my dear friend/editor/sounding board, Anne Gehris, who read and reviewed my manuscript; my partner, Chris Clavelli; my daughter, the eternally curious Rafaella; the people of Washington Heights and beyond who supported my experiment in place-based science education, Storefront Science; the children who attend classes with me, especiall my Early Explorers who unwittingly tested so many of the ideas represented in this book; and to Stephanie Roselli and the folks at Gryphon House, Inc., for giving my ideas a home.

BULK PURCHASE

Gryphon House books are available for special premiums and sales promotions as well as for fund-raising use. Special editions or book excerpts also can be created to specifications. For details, contact the Director of Marketing at Gryphon House.

DISCLAIMER

SCIENCE
Not just foR scientists!

**Easy
Explorations
for Young
Children**

Leonisa Ardizzone, EdD

Photography courtesy of Shutterstock.com

GRYPHON HOUSE, INC.
Lewisville, NC

Published by Gryphon House, Inc.

P. O. Box 10, Lewisville, NC 27023

800.638.0928; 877.638.7576 (fax)

Visit us on the web at www.gryphonhouse.com.

Cover photograph courtesy of Shutterstock.com © 2014.

LIBRARY OF CONGRESS CATALOGING-IN-PUBLICATION DATA

Ardizzone, Leonisa, 1968- author.

 Science--not just for scientists! : easy explorations for young children / Leonisa Ardizzone, EdD.

     pages cm

 Includes bibliographical references and index.

 ISBN 978-0-87659-484-1

 1. Science--Juvenile literature. 2. Science--Methodology--Juvenile literature. 3. Science--Study and teaching. I. Title. II. Title: Science, not just for scientists!

 Q163.A783 2014

 500--dc23

                                     2014003143

Table of Contents

SCIENCE—Not Just for Scientists!

INTRODUCTION
WHY SCIENCE MATTERS

You wake up to the alarm clock on your smartphone. You press a remote control that turns on the television. You fall out of bed and review your email while pulling up a favorite tune on your desktop. You amble to the kitchen where you pour a cup from your automatic coffeemaker and pop some vitamins to keep yourself healthy.

All the luxuries we have gotten used to—the fridge, the phone, the Internet—don't seem like luxuries at all. They're so common now that we forget that forward-thinking scientists made all these things possible. The science that you might have dreaded in high school has made your life longer, easier, and healthier.

Science is the force behind innovation, advancement, and progress. Science is the reason we have cured diseases, improved communication, easily traveled to other countries, and even voyaged to heavenly bodies. Clearly, science isn't just about facts we learn in a classroom.

Science is a habit of mind that involves problem solving, critical thinking, and analytical assessment. As citizens, we are asked each day to make decisions from the seemingly mundane—what vegetables to buy—to the more complex—whether to follow a treatment a doctor has suggested—that require some level of scientific understanding. The more informed we are, the better the decisions we make about what we eat, where we live, how we live, what we consume, and so on. Using a scientific mind-set, we are better able to analyze our choices. We are better observers who can see connections, understand where things come from, and predict what effects our choices will have.

At the core of scientific thinking is a quest for truth and understanding. This quest drives innovation. On the path to truth and innovation lie wonder, discovery, and analysis, all three of which are innate to children. This habit of mind—the practice of thinking through problems and questions—must start with young children. Focus on cultivating their developing scientific minds.

Educators and parents will have an easier time integrating science into their students' and children's lives by remembering a few premises:

▶ **Start with open-ended investigation.** Just as scientists start with an inquiry (not an answer), provide children with an open-ended question, a problem to solve, or a design challenge. Give them materials to explore and offer guidance as they investigate. Let them work toward a solution or the development of even more questions.

▶ **Develop children's observation skills.** To prepare students for these open-ended investigations, be sure they understand the primary tool of science: observation. This second premise comes quite naturally to children, but observation must be expanded beyond what children see. They can easily record or verbally share their visual and aural observations. Dependent upon the task, they can feel, smell, and taste. These three senses can be useful even if only asking children to imagine what something might feel like, taste like, or smell like.

▶ **Repeatedly expose children to the practices and concepts of science.** This will increase understanding and enhance the cultivation of the scientific mind. Children absorb a lot, but often they don't grasp concepts on the first pass. Lay a solid foundation with repeat practices—enhancing and diving deeper each time.

▶ **Connect content to children's reality and interests.** Base activities on what is happening in the community; what plants and animals are found locally; and what the children are reading, watching, or talking about. Ask them what they are interested in, and collect their ideas. Base activities and learning units on their input.

▶ **Allow ample time for questioning, exploration, and analysis.** Reward curiosity by encouraging children to ask questions and explore content. Help them analyze their observations and organize their findings. Teach them to sort by a variety of variables such as color, use, sound, or texture. Focus on the process and learn alongside children. For example, if a child wants to know more about roller coasters, don't be afraid of physics. Instead, get some building materials and investigate with her the forces that make roller coasters run.

The importance of science and science education must not be understated. Science plays an important role in global society. Looking toward the future, the demand for science and technology skills in employment is increasing; workers and consumers alike need to understand complex systems and applications of technology. Capitalize on and promote the inherent love of science that children have. Wonder and exploration make life more interesting! The things we don't understand become our inspiration for knowing more.

The important thing is not to stop questioning. Curiosity has its own reason for existing.

—Albert Einstein

ALLOW INQUIRY TO HAPPEN

Because the process of science centers on questioning, it is really important to let inquiry happen. What does that mean? Sometimes when working with children, we want to make sure they are learning something or getting enough information. In a true inquiry space, the process is less about the answers and more about the questions. This can be challenging. A room full of children asking why would make anyone want to respond with a concrete explanation. Take heart in knowing that, eventually, answers will emerge, but the questioning process is just as important, if not more so. A few pointers on questioning:

▶ **Ask open-ended questions.** When observing an object or starting an exploration, keep things simple. Use questions such as, "What do you notice?" "What does it remind you of?" "How is this object used?" "Who do you think invented this?" "What does it have in common with _____?" and "Where might this animal live?" For younger children, open-ended questions can be challenging. To get things flowing, ask some yes-or-no or compare/contrast questions, such as, "Do you have a tail like the rat?" "Is this shell smooth or bumpy?" and "How are these two insects the same?" This is especially useful with children who are just learning to express their ideas and opinions about what they observe.

▶ **Don't stifle their thinking.** Children will surely come up with some outrageous ideas during the inquiry process. Rather than saying, "No, that's not right," ask them why they think that, and see where additional questioning can lead.

▶ **Turn questions back to children.** If a child asks you a question, turn it back to her: "Why do you think that happens?" gives her the chance to engage her scientific thinking.

▶ **Don't be afraid to say, "I don't know."** Instead of this phrase being an end to learning, use it as an opening to deeper exploration. If you get stumped, ask the children, "How can we investigate that further?" Then, work together to find ways to gather more information. This could include additional research, reading books, or inviting a guest speaker to talk with the children.

▶ **Let tangents happen.** While we may want children to focus on the task at hand, sometimes their tangents can lead to very interesting learning. Creating a truly constructivist and play-based learning experience means allowing children to share their thinking and giving them time and space to direct their own learning.

How to Use This Book

This book is meant to be a guide and an inspiration. Adapt the lesson ideas to your comfort level and the abilities and interests of the children. The focus is on process and cultivating scientific thinking. The chapters are organized around themes drawn from *A Framework for K–12 Science Education: Practices, Crosscutting Concepts, and Core Ideas:* patterns, cause and effect, size and scale, change and growth, systems, energy, and how things work. Each chapter provides an introduction to the theme and activities for you to incorporate. Do the activities in any order. Use those that you are most comfortable with or, better yet, those that the children are most interested in. I encourage you to step outside your comfort zone and teach something you've never taught before!

If you feel you don't know enough content, don't worry. Share in the process of learning. Help the children to see the world differently; think creatively and critically; analyze, categorize, and make meaning. Embrace the process of science. Remember, no matter where you are or who you are working with, science can be done. Science isn't facts and figures. It is wonder and exploration. It is asking why and how and generating methods to uncover truth and understanding.

CHAPTER ONE

Patterns

If you take time to observe a young child playing, at some point you will see him organizing and grouping his toys. Children make collections and may call them *families.* They may sort items by shape, size, or color. They may categorize objects to create an orderly system and then find things in the room that "match." They are, in essence, practicing classification and creating patterns. Patterns are everywhere, and very young children seem to intuitively find them and point them out.

In the early childhood curriculum, patterns play an important role and are typically explored through math and the arts. However, patterns are an exceptional way to bring more science into your classroom or home. Patterns are abundant in both nature and the human-built world. A walk down the street or a stroll in the forest presents numerous examples of how humans and nature tend toward order and are oriented in patterns. From the simple—the shape of an elm leaf or of windows—to the complex—the number of pine needles in a bundle or the whorls of fingerprints—patterns are everywhere and provide a gateway into cultivating the scientific mind.

Why are we drawn to patterns, and what functions do they serve? First, patterns help us make sense of the world. They break and sort information into meaningful "chunks," allowing children to generate new understandings. For children, this sorting and organizing helps their awareness of the world and how things work, enabling them to make meaning. Second, understanding patterns sets the groundwork for an awareness of and appreciation for ordering. Understanding order, systems, and increasingly more complex patterns aid in the development of critical thinking. In a busy world where we are bombarded with information, patterns allow us to discern the important from the unimportant, laying the groundwork for informed decision making. And finally, patterns are the basis for our system of classification of living and nonliving things. For example, rocks are organized into three groups and living things into five kingdoms. Why does classification matter? It organizes phenomena, allowing for a systematic method of seeing similarities and differences among living and nonliving things.

Playing with patterns is powerful pedagogy. Together, children and adults can create parallels, analogies, and relationships to understand how the world works and how systems exist. Scientists are continually looking for patterns— this is how they answer some of the most complex questions they pose. These patterns arise through data and observations—of the universe, of animal behavior, or of cells in a Petri dish. Collecting information and seeing what patterns emerge is an important part of scientific practice. As children apply this practice, they will develop their own scientific minds. Ultimately, through making observations, asking questions, creating groupings, and drawing conclusions, children will not only see that they can control their learning but also develop

skills and habits of mind that will serve them for years to come.

Since patterns are accessible for children and tie into topics already part of the early childhood curriculum, adding a science dimension is not difficult. The following activities are designed to tap into the innate pattern-understanding and pattern-making ability of children. They will use scientific thinking and process to make decisions and defend and explain those choices.

The activities do not have to be done in sequence. Use the activity that fits the interest levels of the children you are working with. There is no time frame: The activities can be done for one week or an hour or as a standing exploration in a corner or a table in your classroom or home, allowing children to return to their exploration whenever they would like. Give the children plenty of time and space to explore, and join them in their discoveries!

15

SCIENCE—Not Just for Scientists!

Patterns in Nature

ESSENTIAL QUESTION:

What patterns do we observe in the natural world?

OBJECTIVES:

▶ Children will explore patterns by examining and classifying objects from nature.

▶ They will create collections based on characteristics they observe.

MATERIALS:

flowers

insects (preserved in resin or glass)

leaves

magnifying glasses

pebbles

pinecones

preserved plants and animals

rocks

shells

METHODS:

1. Place the specimens on a large table where the children can observe. Alternatively, you can create collection boxes, and place them on tables for the children to work with in small groups. You could also create the collection together by gathering samples on a walk in your local environment or by having the children bring in something from home.

EASTERN REDBUD
Cercis canadensis

2. Ask the children, "What are all these things?" Give them all time to name what they see.

3. Give them magnifying glasses, and encourage them to see details.

4. When possible, let them feel the objects and describe the textures. Elicit details from them: "a rock" could become "a gray, sparkly rock."

5. Encourage them to compare items to other objects in the group, in the room, or at home.

6. Have the children make groups of two to five items based on characteristics the items have in common. You may have to guide them with a characteristic. Groupings can be based on color, texture, shape, habitat, sound, smell, function, and so on. Take photos of their groupings for display.

7. Have them explain their groupings: "All of these have lines running through them." "All of these are fuzzy." "All of these live in water." Discuss and reflect on their observations and groups. If possible, take video or audio recordings of the children explaining their groupings.

8. Continue making groupings using a variety of characteristics. Use their descriptions whenever possible, but also lead them.

9. Guide the children to the connections between two groups—for example, "These two groups are based on color, and these two are based on texture."

10. Guide the children to understand that objects may belong in more than one group. For example, a bunch of pine needles is both spiky and green. A seashell is spotty and smooth. Begin a discussion of how objects have many characteristics and therefore can be grouped in different ways. For children who are ready for a challenge, help them complete a Venn diagram to illustrate how two disparate groups may create a third group with characteristics in common.

11. To check for understanding, you can have the children play Name that Characteristic! Two to three children can create a grouping, and the other children have to guess what the items have in common.

Patterns in Our Neighborhood

METHODS:

1. Show the children pictures of shapes. For very young children, just seeing the pictures and hearing the names is fine. They do not need to know their shapes before going on the walk.

2. Prepare the children for a neighborhood walk. Explain to them that they will be observers, hunting for shapes, forms, and patterns. Give them clipboards, a Field Guide for Neighborhood Walk, a Field Guide to Shapes, and a pencil or crayon.

ESSENTIAL QUESTION:
What patterns do we see in our neighborhood?

OBJECTIVES:

▶ Children will explore patterns by examining their local environment.

▶ They will begin to identify shapes and forms.

▶ They will generate questions about their observations.

MATERIALS:
binoculars
cameras
clipboards
Field Guide for
    Neighborhood Walk
Field Guide to Shapes
paper
pencils or crayons

20

3. Take a walk. This could be as simple as a stroll around the block or school or a short walk down the street.

4. As you walk, ask the children to notice the structures around them. Look at sidewalk slabs, windows, bricks, fences, doors, and so on. Ask the children to recall the shapes you talked about earlier. Do they see any of those shapes in the structures? What patterns do they see?

5. When they see something interesting, allow them to stop to record what they see. For example, if a child says he sees a circle, he can write, "Circle on school," or he can simply draw a picture. The key is that the children notice details around them, not that they accurately record everything they notice. **Tip:** If you have a camera, take pictures of what they point out and make prints for later use.

6. Upon returning from the neighborhood walk, ask the children to share their data. Talk with them about the shapes and patterns they noticed. Create charts with their findings—for example, how many rectangles, how many windows, and so on.

7. Give the children the photos you took, and let them create groupings and patterns of the photos of what they saw on the walk.

Table 2.1			
FIELD GUIDE TO SHAPES			
Name			
Shape	Shape Name	How Many Do You See?	Where?
 ▭			
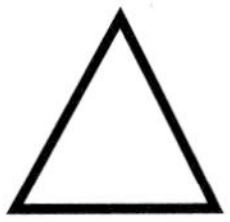 △			
◻			
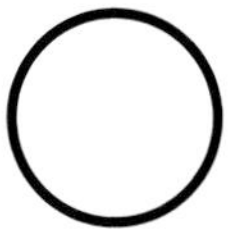 ◯			

VARIATIONS:

▸ Have the children identify living and nonliving things on a walk. What evidence do they see of these things? How do they know if something is living or nonliving?

▸ Create a scavenger hunt for the children to do on a walk. Give them a checklist of things to look for. When they are comfortable with the scavenger hunt, they can create their own lists for friends or family members to complete.

Table 2.2		
FIELD GUIDE FOR NEIGHBORHOOD WALK		
Name		
Date and time of observations:		
Count or draw what you see:		
Trees	Other Plants	Animals
List, draw, and describe the shapes and sizes of what you see:		
Draw specific structures and specimens here:		

Patterns in the Sky: Clouds

PATTERNS—Chapter One

ESSENTIAL QUESTION:

What patterns exist in the sky?

OBJECTIVE:

Children will examine clouds to identify similarities and differences.

MATERIALS:

clipboards
digital camera
images of types of clouds
markers or crayons
paper

METHODS:

1. Take the children outside and observe the clouds. Provide them with paper, markers or crayons, and clipboards. Encourage them to draw their observations. Continue this for as many days as you would like. Try to do it at the same time each day. Date each drawing for later use.

2. After they have observed the sky for a few days, help them organize their drawings in date order and ask them to describe what they see. Do the clouds look the same every day? Are they different shapes or different colors? What characteristics do they have? Are they tall, short, fluffy, silky, and so on? Help them to see that their scientific observations are leading to the establishment of a pattern.

3. On another day, present a cloud chart to the children, or take a look at a website that features photos of different types of clouds, such as http://cloudappreciationsociety. org. Encourage the children to try to match their cloud observations to the pictures.

4. As they make the connection between their own observations and the types of clouds on charts, ask them to make predictions of what clouds they may see over the next few days.

23

SCIENCE—Not Just for Scientists!

Patterns in the Sky: Solar System

ESSENTIAL QUESTION:

What patterns exist in the sky?

OBJECTIVE:

Children will notice details of planets and the moon.

MATERIALS:

markers or crayons
paper
photos of the moon and
   planets

METHODS:

1. Show the children a picture of the moon. Ask them what it is. Have them describe what they see. Encourage them to describe it in as much detail as possible. To help them use their observation skills, ask them what they think it would smell, taste, feel, and sound like.

2. Show them pictures taken from space of Earth and of other planets in our solar system. Ask some open-ended questions:
   ▶ Where are these things?
   ▶ How can we take pictures of them?
   ▶ What lives there?
   ▶ Have you ever visited there?

3. Ask them to describe each planet in terms of all their senses:
   ▶ What do you think it tastes like?
   ▶ What does it smell like?
   ▶ Do you think it has a sound? What sort of sound does it make?
   ▶ What do you think it feels like?
   ▶ Create a chart to record their observations.

4. Ask them to notice particular similarities and differences among the planets and moon, such as color, size, and so on.

5. Using the photos, create a "map" on the floor or wall of the solar system. The aim here is for them to see that the planets are interrelated and that they create a pattern.

ACTIVITIES AND APPLICATIONS

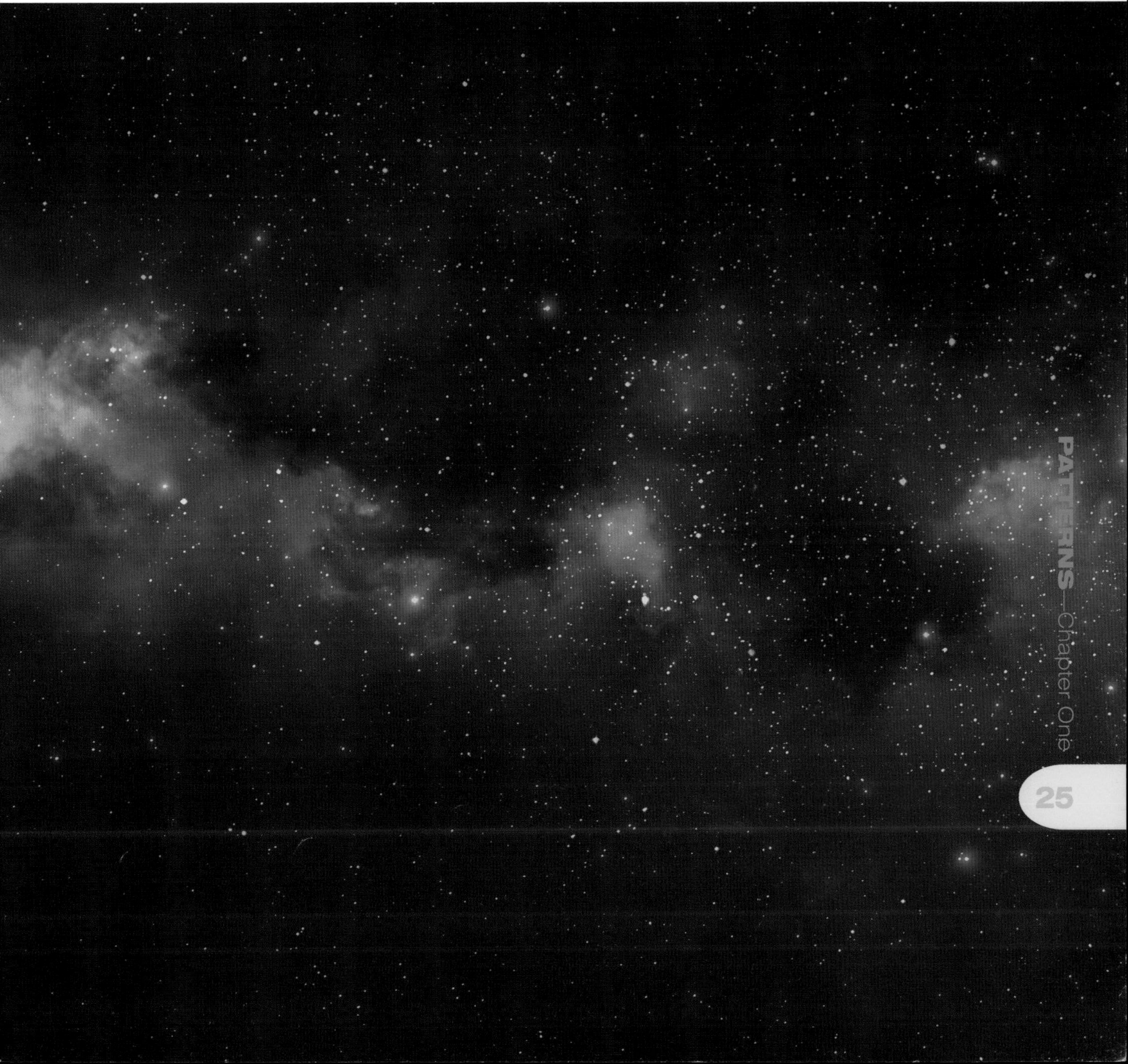

SCIENCE—Not Just for Scientists!

Patterns in the Sky: Constellations

ESSENTIAL QUESTION:

What patterns exist in the sky?

OBJECTIVE:

Children will notice details of constellations.

MATERIALS:

images of constellations, such as the Little Dipper, the Big Dipper, and Andromeda

markers or crayons

paper

METHODS:

1. Give the children blank sheets of paper and a single marker or crayon. Ask them to make dots on the page in any way they choose.

2. Ask them to exchange sheets with a neighbor (only if they want to) and then connect the dots to make images of animals, people, seashells, trees, or anything else they wish.

3. When they are finished, ask them to share their dot-to-dot pictures. Ask them to discuss how they made their choices. Why did they pick those animals or people? Was it hard or easy to connect the dots?

4. Show children pictures of the night sky. Ask them what they see. Ask them to share what they know about stars.

5. Ask them how they think people can remember the names of all these stars. People looked at the stars and saw pictures there. That is how they kept track of the stars in the sky. Ask volunteers to trace a figure in the stars like the ones they created on paper. Introduce the word *constellation:* "a pattern created by linking stars together into a picture."

6. Show them pictures of the most commonly understood constellations, such as the Little Dipper, the Big Dipper, Andromeda, and so on, so they can see how "sky pictures" were created. A useful site for images of several constellations can be found at http://stars.astro.illinois.edu/sow/const.html.

7. Ask them to look at the dot-to-dot pictures they created. Encourage them to name their "constellations" and create their own stories about them, if they wish.

8. If they can, ask them to watch the night sky and tell a grown-up what they see.

SCIENCE—Not Just for Scientists!

Patterns We Create

ESSENTIAL QUESTION:

How do we create patterns every day?

OBJECTIVE:

Children will create patterns with sound and objects.

MATERIALS:

assorted found objects, such as blocks or toy cars

colored paper

drums

kazoos

maracas

markers

paper

METHODS:

1. Draw a few shape patterns, and ask the children to help you figure out what comes next for each—for example,

2. Encourage the children to create their own patterns with objects in the room, such as blocks, pieces of colored paper, and so on. Encourage them to draw patterns on paper.

3. Once they understand the idea of a visual repeating pattern, tell them they can make an *aural* pattern: a pattern of sounds. Introduce a simple rhythmic pattern, such as slap-slap (on thighs), clap-clap. They can repeat it over and over.

4. Encourage the children to make new aural patterns. To inspire them, use their names as a springboard. For example, for the name *Tiffany,* a child could clap on the first syllable, snap on the second, and slap her thighs on the third. Let the children explore creating patterns from their names and learning each other's name patterns.

5. Continuing with the aural idea, in small groups, have the children select a musical instrument or noisemaker of some kind. Maracas made from sand or rice in an empty potato-chip can work well, as do simple drums made from empty coffee cans with the lids safely sealed on. Let them explore creating repeating musical patterns.

6. Encourage them to share their patterns with their friends and ask their friends to guess what comes next in the pattern. As they explore, talk with them: "Henry, you made a clap-clap-clap-snap pattern." "Where else have you heard patterns like this?"

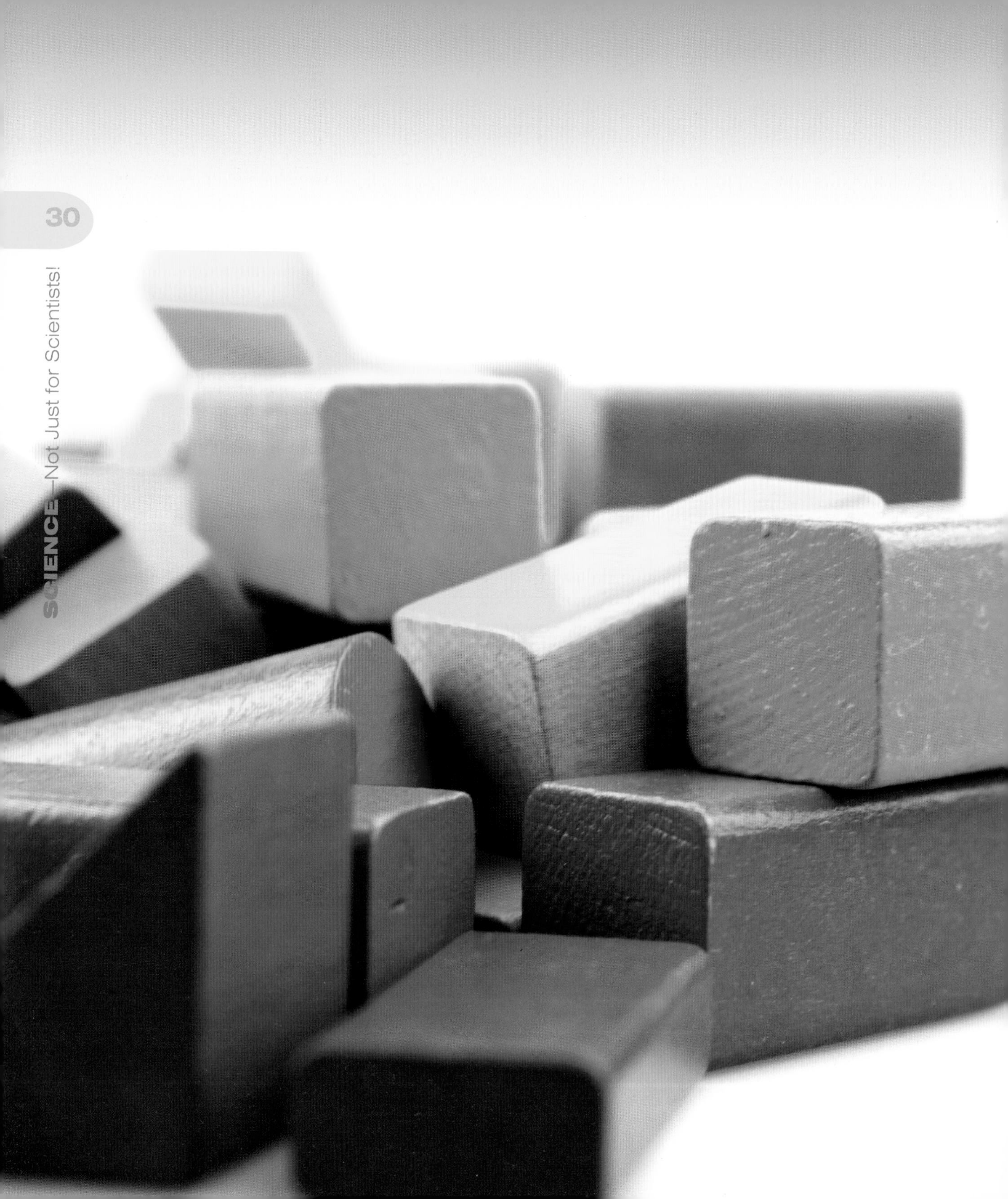

CHAPTER TWO

Cause and Effect

At a very young age, children learn the principle of cause and effect. They cry; they get attention. They drop something, and it breaks. They bang a pot, and it makes noise. Through their own observations, they begin to make a connection between actions and reactions. They might not be able to articulate that connection when they are very young, but the awareness is there, and as they get older, they will begin to explain what they see. Better yet, they will begin to ask increasingly more complex questions to understand their observations.

In many ways, human relationships and consequences are the earliest basis for children to understand cause and effect. A child acts, and if it is a not-so-good action, a consequence follows. If she does something well, she gets praise or a reward. Their behavior and the behavior of those around them teach them about connections, about cause and effect. Science investigation involves the study of relationships. Phenomena have causes, and scientists attempt to unearth what those causes are. They also try to explain the effects of actions and inputs. Children also study relationships. They observe and mimic. They repeat activities to see if they get the same results. They try to understand why things happen.

Watch a child playing with blocks, and you will see her build, then destroy, then build again with slight changes. She will test as she goes along—determining strength or stability. She may not be aware that what she is doing is experimental. To a child, it is play. But through play, children practice science and use the analytical and problem-solving methods involved in science and engineering. Through cause and effect, children learn to make observations and predictions; they learn why something happens. Examining and analyzing causal connections teaches children how to make predictions. This is an early step in scientific inquiry.

Exploration of cause and effect is the basis of experimental design and fosters analytical thinking. Scientists manipulate variables based on a question, to study outcomes. Playing with cause and effect is the beginning of an eventually more methodical means of designing and conducting experiments. As children grow and develop more intricate thought processes, they will develop more advanced questions for exploration that will necessitate more complex forms of experimentation. Manipulating variables at a young age and seeing different results is the start of this type of inquiry.

Cultivate the analytical exploration of cause and effect by giving children plenty of room for experimentation: If I change a variable (A), then what happens? Give children time to analyze their findings, even something as simple as why a plant grew better on the windowsill than in the refrigerator. Allow them the time to articulate their observations and develop an explanation for what they believe occurred. They will be making connections—just like scientists do!

How High?

ESSENTIAL QUESTION:

How do balls of different materials behave when dropped from various heights?

OBJECTIVE:

Children will examine the principle of cause and effect by testing the bounce of different balls.

MATERIALS:

a collection of balls, such as Ping-Pong, golf, tennis, rubber, wooden, and so on

marker

meter sticks, rulers, or tape measures

paper

paper strips, cut to 10 centimeters or 1 meter

NOTE:

In this lesson, measurement is done with metric units. Most scientific study is done with metric units, so it is a good idea to get children started in this system when they are young.

METHODS:

1. Ask the children to name items that bounce. Make a list of their ideas.
2. Ask them if these bouncy things will bounce anywhere. Ask them what factors might affect how high something bounces. Let them share their ideas.
3. If you are working with a large group, place the children in groups of two to four.
4. Provide each group with four or five different kinds of balls. Be sure that each group has a variety of balls, some that bounce well and some that do not. Examine the collection with the children, and discuss what material each ball is made of.

33

SCIENCE—Not Just for Scientists!

5. Give the children a measurement tool, such as a ruler, meter stick, or tape measure. For younger children or children who may not know how to read rulers, give them strips of paper of a premeasured length, such as 10 centimeters or 1 meter.

6. Encourage the children to bounce the balls to see which ones bounce highest. Encourage them use different amounts of force to bounce the balls.

7. After they have completed their exploration, give the children copies of the data table.

Table 3.1		
DATA COLLECTION: BALLS (EXPLORATORY)		
Name		
Partner		
Type of Ball	How Many Bounces?	How High?

Table 3.2			
DATA COLLECTION: BALLS (SPECIFIC)			
Name			
Partner			
Type of Ball	Starting Height	Bounces: Surface 1	Bounces: Surface 2

8. Have them drop each ball from a set height, such as 3 feet. Help them record their observations.

9. After experimentation, encourage them to share their findings. Ask questions that allow them to develop an understanding about the relationship between ball material and bounce: "Which ball bounced the highest? What is it made of? Which ones did not bounce high? What are they made of?"

SCIENCE—Not Just for Scientists!

ESSENTIAL QUESTION:

How does temperature effect how color moves through water?

OBJECTIVE:

Children will explore cause and effect by observing how food coloring responds to water of different temperatures.

MATERIALS:

clear, unbreakable
    containers
cold tap water
hot tap water (adult only)
liquid food coloring,
    green or blue
room-temperature tap
    water
thermometers
very cold water (0–5°C)
very hot water (adult only)
warm tap water

What Color Is Your Water?

METHODS:

1. Fill the containers with water of varying temperatures, and line them up on a table.
2. Gather the children around the table. Encourage them to look carefully at the jars: Do all the jars look the same? Can they tell which are hot or cold? (They can carefully touch the outsides of the jars.)
3. If the children are new to using thermometers, take time here to discuss why we use thermometers and how they work. (**Tip:** A resource on how a thermometer works: http://home.howstuffworks.com/therm.htm.) Measure the temperature of the water in each container.
4. Ask the children to predict what will happen when you drop food coloring into each jar.

5. Observe what happens when you add a drop of food coloring to each jar. Drop only one drop into each jar.

6. Observe the water. Ask the children what is happening to the color. Is it spreading out? Is it floating? Is it sinking? Is the water changing color?

7. Wait for one minute, then observe again. What changes do the children notice?

8. Wait for two minutes, then observe. What changes do the children notice?

9. Wait for two more minutes, then observe. What changes do the children notice?

10. Did the food coloring behave like they predicted it would? Encourage them to develop opinions about the movement of the food coloring in the water.

Note

Use a Celsius thermometer. The range of 0 to 100° is easier for children to understand than Fahrenheit. **Note:** To get the water (0–5°C) this cold, put crushed ice in it, then remove the ice. Boil the water first to make it very hot.

SCIENCE—Not Just for Scientists!

ESSENTIAL QUESTION:

How does location affect plant growth?

OBJECTIVES:

▶ Children will explore the concept of variables by designing a plant growth experiment.

▶ Children will predict the effects of variables on plant growth.

MATERIALS:

light source

marker

paper

paper cups or sod pots

seeds (rye grass works well)

soil

water

Where Will I Grow Best?

METHODS:

1. Ask the children what plants need to grow. Write down their thoughts.

2. Ask what would happen if the plants grew without these things. Record their ideas and predictions.

3. Discuss the idea of a *variable*, a factor or element that can be changed. Tell the children that they will be manipulating variables to see the effects these changes have on plant growth.

4. Make a list of what they would like to change, such as the amount of light, the temperature, the amount of water, the amount of soil, and so on.

5. Help them set up their experiments: Put soil in cups, then add seeds. They can then determine what variable(s) they will examine.

6. Set up a control cup, which will get soil, seeds, and water and will be placed in sunlight.

7. Label each cup with the variable(s) that the children are studying—for example, No Light, Lots of Water, or No Soil. Older children can add their ideas to a data chart.

8. Each day, encourage the children to check their cups and record or share their observations. Talk with them about what they notice.

Table 3.3				
DATA COLLECTION: SOIL OBSERVATION				
Name				
Partner				
Draw or write your observations:				
Variable	1: Date	2: Date	3: Date	4: Date

SCIENCE—Not Just for Scientists!

Rolling Downhill

ESSENTIAL QUESTION:

How can the angle of a ramp affect the motion of a marble?

OBJECTIVES:

▶ Children will create ramps of different heights to examine the motion of a marble.

▶ Children will predict how the marbles will be affected by the angles of the ramps.

MATERIALS:

blocks

marbles

scrap wood molding

METHODS:

1. Ask the children if any of them ride a bike, trike, or scooter. Ask them if they go faster moving uphill or downhill. Why do they think this happens?

2. In an area with lots of floor space, provide the children with wood molding, blocks, and marbles. Let them play with the marbles for a little while.

3. Encourage them to set up the molding as ramps, using the blocks to vary the height.

4. Ask them to predict how the height of the ramp will affect the speed of the marble.

5. Let them test their predictions. Talk with them about what they observe.

6. Have them compare their designs and outcomes with one another. For older children, they can collect data on how fast or how far their marble travels on ramps of different heights.

SCIENCE—Not Just for Scientists!

Chain Reactions

ESSENTIAL QUESTION:

How can we observe cause and effect?

OBJECTIVES:

▶ Children will create simple cardboard contraptions to demonstrate a chain reaction.

▶ Children will build a game or machine of their own design.

MATERIALS:

beanbags

cardboard boxes and sheets

child-safe scissors

heavy paper

marbles or balls

markers and crayons

pipe cleaners

straws

tape

METHODS:

1. Set up a small chain reaction for children to observe. You can make it simple or elaborate. For example, set up a few dominoes that, when knocked over, push over a small cup that releases a small ball that rolls and lands in a cardboard box on the floor. Get creative!

2. Invite the children to reset the chain reaction and trigger it again. Ask them to say out loud what they observe happening and why they think it works.

3. Ask them to invent a similar game that their friends can play.

4. If you have a large group, create smaller groups of children or let them work alone or in pairs if they wish. Give them the materials, and allow plenty of time for them to explore, experiment, and invent. Let them use their imaginations! This activity can be done over multiple days, and they can continue to fine-tune their inventions.

5. When they are ready, let them demonstrate their contraptions.

CHAPTER THREE

Size and Scale

Being small makes the world seem so very big! Most children are in awe of very large things. They are curious about dinosaurs, skyscrapers, and the solar system, all of which are significantly larger than they are. Understanding size can be abstract for young children. Ask them how big dinosaurs are, and the response will probably be, "Gigantic!" How can we help them understand *size*, measurement as an absolute value, and *scale*, size as a relative concept?

Children already have a sense of size and scale. Through their toys—building blocks, a dollhouse, and action figures—they have a feel for how things fit. When they build a Lego structure, they know that it is not the same as a real building. They understand that it is a model, even though they do not comprehend what the proportions are. When playing with dolls or action figures, they can see that the Calico Critters are much too small for the Barbie house, and Barbie cannot fit into the Calico Critter house. As parents and educators, we can help them translate this sense of big and small into a real understanding of scale or the relative size of objects.

Children also play with replicas of life-size items. Those toy kitchens they love have been scaled to fit them. They see the

43

difference between the wooden stove in the preschool and the metal one in the kitchen. They recognize that the pans, oven mitts, and fake food are all child-size. So, why not use their play to help them learn more about science?

They experience measurement quite clearly through their own bodies. Most families have growth charts on a wall or markings on a kitchen door to track the heights of their children. Children go to doctors and get weighed and measured, and they can see a record of their growth since birth. They can feel themselves getting bigger in relation to the sizes of their bed, their shoes, or their clothes. Introducing the concepts of size and scale will help young children understand increasingly complex concepts of measurement, ratio, and proportion as they get older.

Big, Small, and In-between

ESSENTIAL QUESTION:

How do we classify objects by size?

OBJECTIVE:

▶ Children will explore relative size by categorizing items in their environment.

MATERIALS:

a variety of very big objects, such as a large shipping box and an area rug

a variety of very small objects, such as grains of sand and seeds

METHODS:

1. Place a collection of items on a table and the surrounding area. Be sure to have items ranging in size from the very small (1 cm or smaller) to the relatively large (about 1 meter).

2. Ask the children to arrange the objects from smallest to largest. Talk with the children about how they sorted the objects. If you have included oddly shaped items, ask older children what dimension, length or depth, they used to determine the size of the object.

3. Ask the children to divide the objects into three or four groups based on similarity in size. Talk with them about how they determined those groupings: Why did they cut off the groups when they did?

4. Give each of the children (or each group, if you are working with several children) an identical object of your choosing. Ask them to identify things nearby that are larger than that object. Discuss the choices they make.

5. Ask them to identify things that are smaller than that object. Discuss the choices they make.

6. Repeat this comparison to the object several times over several days. The children will enjoy comparing new items and talking about how something is larger or smaller than their object.

Who Can Live Here?

ESSENTIAL QUESTION:
What is *scale*?

OBJECTIVE:
▶ Children will explore the concept of scale by creating homes for toys of varying sizes.

MATERIALS:
boxes or construction paper
building toys and materials, such as blocks, Tinker Toys, Legos, Lincoln Logs, cardboard dollhouse or box decorated to resemble a house
dolls, stuffed animals, and action figures in a variety of sizes

METHODS:

1. Select a variety of dolls and toys (have as many as there are children in the group), and place the toys on a table.
2. Ask the children to arrange them from shortest to tallest.
3. Ask, "Would (pick a large toy) and (pick a small toy) make good roommates? Could they live in the same house?" Elicit a discussion on the relative sizes of the two toys.
4. Set a dollhouse (or box decorated as a house) on the table next to the toy figures. Ask the children to determine which figures would be able to live comfortably in the house. Discuss why some figures would fit and some would not, introducing the concept of *scale*.

48

5. Invite the children to look around the room. How big is the door compared to the height of the wall? How big are the windows? How high is the ceiling compared to the children or to a grown-up?

6. In pairs or small groups, encourage the children to use building blocks or other building materials (Tinker Toys, Lincoln Logs, cardboard boxes, construction paper) to design and build a house that will fit one of the figurines. Discuss why they made the choices they did. Ask how they would have to change their house to accommodate a figure of a different size.

Exploring Measurement

ESSENTIAL QUESTION:

How do we measure things?

OBJECTIVE:

▶ Children will measure various objects to begin their understanding of measurement.

MATERIALS:

child-safe scissors

construction paper

crayons or markers

measuring tapes

objects of varying sizes

rulers (one for each child)

METHODS:

1. Give each child paper, scissors, and a crayon or marker. Help each child trace his hand on a piece of paper and cut the tracing out. Make one for yourself, too.

2. Show the children how to use their hand cutouts to measure different objects in the room. Let them explore freely and measure what they are interested in. Encourage them to share their measurements with peers or with a grown-up. Older children can record their data on a chart.

Table 4.1			
DATA COLLECTION: MEASUREMENT			
Name			
Partner			
Object	How Many Hands?	How Many Inches?	How Many Centimeters?

SCIENCE—Not Just for Scientists!

3. Have a few children measure one object, such as a chair or table. Measure the same object with your hand cutout. Compare the measurements. Ask why the measurements are not all the same. Lead the children to the understanding that the hands vary in size, so the measurements will vary, too.

4. Give each child a ruler, and ask them what a ruler is and what it is used for. Have them read the numbers if they can.

5. Have each child first measure his hand cutout. How many centimeters is it? How many inches?

6. Let them move around the room measuring different objects with the ruler. Encourage them to share their findings with a peer or an adult. Children who are ready for a challenge can record their measurements on the chart.

Solar System Walk

Save this activity until the children have an idea of the concepts of relative and absolute size. This activity introduces some really big ideas—they will not fully grasp it all at once, and that is okay! The children will want to return to it again and again as their understanding of relative and absolute size develops.

METHODS:

1. Show the children photos or drawings of the sun and planets. Ask them what they are and what they know about them. Can they name the planets? If you want, you can write the names of the planets in order from the sun on a large paper for them to refer to: Mercury, Venus, Earth, Mars, Jupiter, Saturn, Uranus, and Neptune. (Sorry, Pluto, you're out of there!)

2. Ask the children how far away they think the sun is from Earth. Can we travel there? How long might it take? Listen to their ideas. The aim is to get them thinking about large distances.

3. Create a solar system walk for the children to explore. My favorite version is from *The Thousand-Yard Model or the Earth as a Peppercorn* by Guy Ottewell. Outside or in a large indoor space, choose where you want the center of your solar system model to be. Set down the baseball, and label it as the sun. Proceed as follows:

   ◗ With the children, walk ten paces (counting as you go) and stop. Set down a mustard seed and label it as Mercury.

   ◗ Walk nine paces and set down a peppercorn. Label it as Venus.

ESSENTIAL QUESTION:

How big is the solar system?

OBJECTIVE:

◗ Children will develop an understanding of scale by creating a walking map of our solar system.

MATERIALS:

2 peanuts or coffee beans

2 peppercorns

3 mustard or poppy seeds (or similarly tiny seeds)

baseball

box or container to carry everything in

chart depicting the solar system

chestnut or pecan

hazelnut or acorn

paper labels: sun, Mercury, Venus, Earth, Mars, Jupiter, Saturn, Uranus, Neptune

photos of the sun and planets

▶ Walk seven paces and set down another peppercorn. Label it as Earth.

▶ Walk fourteen paces and place another mustard seed. Label it as Mars.

4. So far, you have covered the inner planets. Now comes a lot of walking! Along the way, include the children in a discussion about the distance: "How far are we walking?"

▶ With the children, walk ninety-five paces and set down a chestnut or pecan. Label it as Jupiter.

▶ Walk 112 paces and place a hazelnut or acorn. Label it as Saturn.

▶ Walk 249 paces and place a peanut or coffee bean. Label it as Uranus.

▶ Walk 281 paces and set down another peanut or coffee bean. Label it as Neptune.

5. Look back at your model of our solar system. Ask the children what it tells them about the distances of the planets. Talk with them about the sizes of the planets as compared with the sun. Which is the largest planet? How big is Earth compared to the sun?

Used with permission from Guy Ottewell, www.universalworkshop.com.

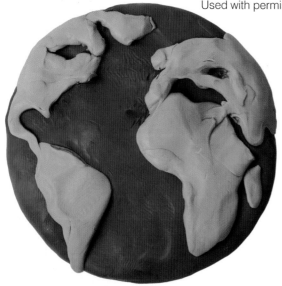

Incredible Shrinking Food

METHODS:

1. Place a collection of fruits and vegetables on the table. Give the children time to share their observations of the items.
2. Cut samples of each item into similarly sized pieces. Using a triple beam balance or a small scale, work with the children to determine the mass of each of the items. Record the data on a chart.
3. As you are weighing the items, verbalize each step you take. Let the children use the instrument, too.
4. Place each item in its own plastic container and cover with a lid.

ESSENTIAL QUESTION:

How can we use measurement to observe change?

OBJECTIVE:

▶ Children will use a balance or scale to determine the mass or weight of various food items.

MATERIALS:

chart paper
marker
plastic containers with
lids
variety of fruits and
vegetables, such as
cucumber, squash,
lettuce, apple, banana,
orange, kiwi, tomato,
and so on

5. Weigh each item plus the container. Record this information on the chart. (If children are learning subtraction, use this as an opportunity for them to determine the mass of the container.)

6. Ask the children what they think will happen to the fruits and veggies in one day, in one week, and in one month. Set the containers aside for a day.

7. The next day, ask the children to observe the appearance of the items in the containers. Record any changes they see. Weigh the samples again, and record the results.

8. Repeat this each day or whenever the children are interested. Talk with the children about the changes they notice.

9. As time progresses, the food will begin to rot. Liquid will begin to leave certain fruits and vegetables. When you weigh the items, you can do one of two things: make the measurement in the container, thus weighing all the water that is escaping—and the mass will stay relatively the same, or not include any excess liquid in the measurement, so the children can see the mass of the item changing. Your choice!

CHAPTER FOUR

Change and Growth

Heraclitus, a philosopher of ancient Greece, said, "Nothing endures but change." Change is everywhere. Children see day turn to night and summer turn to fall. They recognize that they are getting taller and witness their bodies developing. They watch houses being built or remark on their parents getting grey hair. Change is constantly in their realm of observation. Embrace the topic of change, and use it as a rich learning opportunity.

Children probably observe that change is not random. As they grow out of clothes, they recognize that others do the same. They can see that their growth is a progression, possibly marked on a kitchen doorway. Each evening they see the moon come out, and they safely assume that it will be there again the next night. We can take children's intuitive understanding of change and help them learn that change is often part of a pattern. Both growth and change are unifying principles in science that can help children make sense of the world.

SCIENCE—Not Just for Scientists!

Tracking Our Shadows

ESSENTIAL QUESTION:

How do shadows grow?

OBJECTIVES:

▸ The children will develop an understanding of the motion of the Earth relative to the sun.

▸ The children will develop an understanding of how the Earth is moving by observing a shadow study.

MATERIALS:

chalk

clipboards

lamp or flashlight

markers

measuring devices (tape measure, meter stick, or premeasured strips of paper)

paper or data tables

METHODS:

1. Using a lamp or flashlight, encourage the children to make shadow puppets against a wall. Have no more than two children casting shadows at a time. Ask the children to discuss what they see: How big do the shadows appear? What details do you see or not see? Let each child have a turn.

2. During the shadow play, ask the children to move their hands closer to and farther from the light source. What changes do they notice? Why does this happen? Listen to their ideas. Manipulate the light source to change the angle of the light on their hands. Again, have the children discuss what they are seeing.

3. With this shadow idea fresh in their minds, ask them when they see shadows outside. What is the light source? Do shadows always appear the same? Listen to their ideas.

4. Designate a set time that you can go outside every day for at least a week. The first day may take longer than the others, but eventually the activity should only need fifteen to twenty minutes. Be sure that your location is in the sun, so that the children's bodies will cast shadows. Give each child a piece of chalk, and encourage pairs of children to trace around each other's shadows. If it is a grassy area, give them tape measures and have them measure their shadows. **Tip:** If you have a camera, take photos of the children with their shadows.

5. Once they have drawn their shadows, have them measure the lengths of the shadows with a tape measure. Ask them to observe where the sun is in the sky each day.

6. Older children can record their data on a table.

7. Repeat this activity every day at the same time in the same spot for a week or longer if you can. The longer you do it, the richer your results will be. Each day, ask the children to make observations about the lengths and shapes of the shadows. What is happening to their shadows? What is changing? Why?

8. When the shadow study is complete, discuss the position of the sun in sky—its relation to the horizon—and the lengths of the shadows. You can return to the flashlight shadow play to have them explore how to manipulate the shadows by moving the light source.

Table 4.1									
DATA COLLECTION: SHADOWS									
Name									
Partner									
Time of Observation									
Length of Shadow:									
Day 1	Day 2	Day 3	Day 4	Day 5	Day 6	Day 7	Day 8	Day 9	Day 10

SCIENCE—Not Just for Scientists!

Chemical Change

ESSENTIAL QUESTION:

What happens when chemicals react?

OBJECTIVES:

▶ Children will conduct simple chemical combinations.

▶ Children will observe reactions and outcomes.

MATERIALS:

3 beakers or transparent plastic cups

baking soda solution (1 Tbsp. baking soda mixed with 1 Tbsp. water)

graduated cylinder or large jar

plastic tablecloth or drop cloth

water

white vinegar

METHODS:

1. Fill one beaker or transparent plastic cup halfway with water. Set the cup on a table.

2. Fill another beaker or transparent plastic cup halfway with white vinegar. Set the cup on the table next to the first cup.

3. Fill the third beaker or transparent plastic cup halfway with baking soda solution. Set the cup on the table with the others.

4. Without allowing them to touch or smell the cups, ask the children to guess what is in each container. Ask them what information they used to decide.

5. Tell them what the substances are, and talk about each one. What do the children know about water, vinegar, and baking soda? Ask them to predict what will happen if the liquids are combined. How do they know?

6. In a graduated cylinder or large jar (the graduated cylinder makes a particularly exciting and messy demonstration), pour the water, then the vinegar, and finally the baking soda solution. What happens? Ask the children to share their observations. Why does it overflow? What do they think the bubbles are made of? (Hint: The bubbles are filled with carbon dioxide. Compare these bubbles to those in fizzy drinks.)

7. For added fun and interest, let the children experiment with different ratios of baking soda to water in their baking soda solutions. What happens in the exploration when they change the ratio?

WHY DO THEY FIZZ?

Vinegar contains acetic acid, an acid (that is what makes it taste sour). Baking soda contains sodium bicarbonate, a base. When these two substances are combined, a two-step reaction takes place:

1. They combine to produce carbonic acid.
2. Carbonic acid quickly decomposes into carbon dioxide, sodium acetate, and water.

That two-step reaction causes the fizz!

Sprouts!

ESSENTIAL QUESTION:

How does a seed change into a plant?

OBJECTIVE:

▶ Children will observe how a seed germinates.

MATERIALS:

paper towels
permanent marker
small paper cups
small plastic bags or empty CD jewel cases
soil
transparent containers, such as jars or plastic cups
variety of seeds, such as zucchini, peas, bush beans, beets, or zinnias
water

METHODS:

1. Help the children sort the seeds based on size, shape, color, or texture. Let them share their observations about the seeds.

2. Ask them what seeds are. What do they become? How does that happen? What conditions do the seeds need to grow? Allow the children to share any prior knowledge and theories they have.

3. Help the children create three different environments for the seeds. For the first environment, give each child a CD case or resealable plastic bag, a damp paper towel, and a few seeds. Place the paper towel into the CD case or bag. Place the seeds on the paper towel and seal the case. Label the bag or case with the child's name and the date. Let the child decide the best place to put the bag or case so the seeds will grow. The bags need not be all in the same location.

4. Help the children fill small paper cups with soil. Label the cups. Let them put the seeds in the soil, add water, and place the cups in a different location from the CD cases or bags.

5. Give each child a transparent container. Help them fill the containers with soil, add some seeds, and water. Label the containers. Place these in a third location.

6. Over time, encourage the children to examine their cases, cups, and containers. What changes do they notice? Do they notice differences? Do some locations seem to be better for the seeds than others? Why do they think so?

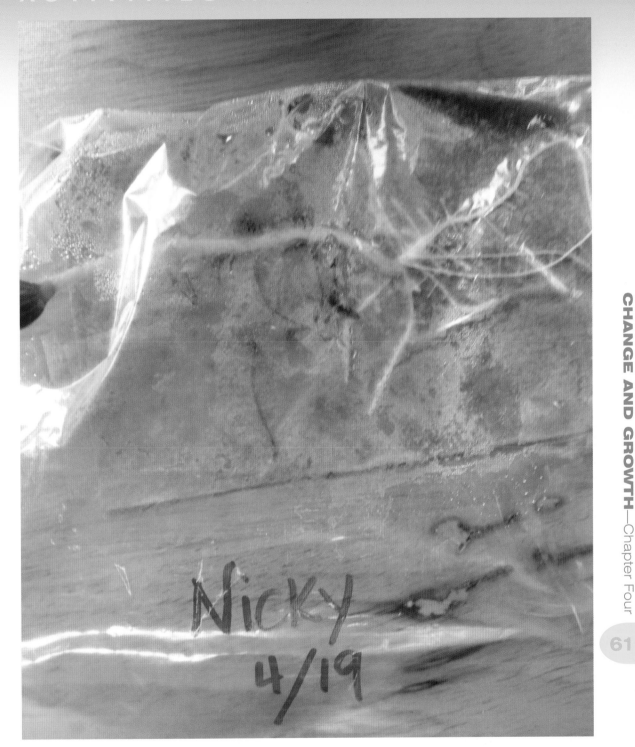

SCIENCE—Not Just for Scientists!

Yum! Butter!

ESSENTIAL QUESTION:

How does milk become butter?

OBJECTIVE:

▸ Children will observe a physical reaction through the process of making butter.

MATERIALS:

heavy cream
plastic containers with tight lids
samples of butter

METHODS:

1. Show the children a sample of butter. Ask them what it is. Do they know what butter is made of? How is it made? Who eats it? Let them share what they know. Optional: Have a butter tasting. Place small amounts of butter on crackers, and let the children share their observations about the taste and texture.

2. Show the children the heavy cream, and ask the same questions: What is it made of? How is it made? Who eats it?

3. Pour ¼ cup cream into each container, and tightly close the lid.

4. Pair the children, and give each pair a cream-filled container. Instruct them to shake the jar vigorously but carefully. They can take turns, shaking for one minute or until their arms get tired. They can also occasionally take a break and observe what is happening in the container.

5. Once the cream starts to thicken, they will have made whipped cream. But, they are not done yet! They will eventually see and feel the butter form. Let them remove the lid periodically to observe the stages of the process.

6. When the butter forms, they can conduct the taste test again. Yum!

7. If there is interest, let them try the same process with other kinds of "milk": rice milk, soy milk, almond milk, skim milk, and so on. Does it work? Why or why not?

Teeny Tiny Yeast

ESSENTIAL QUESTION:
What makes bread rise?

OBJECTIVE:

▶ Children will explore the idea of change by designing an experiment to see how yeast works.

METHODS:

1. Show the children a piece of leavened bread and a piece of unleavened bread (matzo). Ask them to share their observations: What is similar about the two? What is different? Let them try to list the main ingredients in each.

2. Talk about what makes the bread "fluffy." Gather their ideas on why and how this happens.

3. Write the word *yeast* on the paper. Ask the children what yeast is. Give them a little information to start their experimentation:

   ▶ Yeast is a tiny living organism—it is a fungus. Do they know other kinds of fungus? Yeast "eats" sugar: it consumes sugar for energy.

MATERIALS:

chart paper
marker
packages of active dry yeast
piece of unleavened bread (matzo)
piece of white or wheat bread
small plastic cups
sugar
water

▶ Yeast produces carbon dioxide, which is the same gas that makes the bubbles of fizzy drinks.

4. Place about 1/8 teaspoon of dry yeast in each cup. Pair up the children or place them in small groups. Give each pair or group a cup of yeast. Give them time to observe the yeast. What do they notice?

5. Place a small amount of sugar in cups for each group. Give the children the sugar and some small cups of water. Let them add a little sugar and a little water to their cups.

6. Ask them to observe what happens in the yeast cups. Record their observations on the chart.

7. Let the yeast cups sit for fifteen minutes. Encourage the children to observe them again. What do they notice? Record their observations. Continue observing the yeast mixtures over time and recording the changes.

8. Optional: For a fun follow-up, add flour to the yeast and let the children watch the dough rise. Bake some simple bread, if you wish.

CHAPTER FIVE

Energy

Children are balls of energy. Spend fifteen minutes with a four-year-old, and you will understand the definition of *nonstop*. How do we begin to engage children in a discussion of energy? Many young children wonder aloud questions such as, "How does my body work?" "What makes me go?" "Why do we eat?" "What makes the light work?" "How does the car or subway run?" "What does the sun do?" The curiosity is there—we just need to create an inquiry process for them to begin to examine the idea of energy.

With young children, keep the concept of energy simple. Worry less about terminology and focus more on big ideas and processes. Introducing these fundamental principles through play sets the groundwork for deeper understanding as they grow older. Focus on three main concepts around energy:

- Energy cannot be created nor destroyed.
- Energy changes form.
- Energy flows.

Keep the activities open ended, and see where the children's questions and explorations lead.

SCIENCE—Not Just for Scientists!

Energy Path

ESSENTIAL QUESTION:

Can we trace the path of energy through our day?

OBJECTIVE:

▶ Children will create a flow chart of energy traveling through their day.

MATERIALS:

markers

paper

photos of items that use energy, such as a light bulb, battery, refrigerator, car, person, plant, and so on

METHODS:

1. Ask the children what they know about energy. What is it? The children may offer ideas such as how things go, how things get warm, and so on.

2. Ask them where we can see energy in action. What uses energy? Encourage them to offer examples, such as light bulbs, the sun, a fire, and so on. You may have to help them with this list.

3. Show them photos of items that use energy. Talk with them about the energy that each item uses.

4. Work with children to create a flow chart of how energy travels through their day. On a sheet of paper, start with waking up:

   ▶ What wakes them? (alarm clock, sun, parent)

   ▶ They eat breakfast. What makes that happen? (refrigerator, stove, parent)

   ▶ They travel to school. How do they get there? (bus, walking, car, bicycle)

Continue in this manner, listing all the items and people that use energy during a typical day. Along the way, gather their observations of how energy is present in every aspect of their lives. Collect questions that they have about energy that you can all explore further.

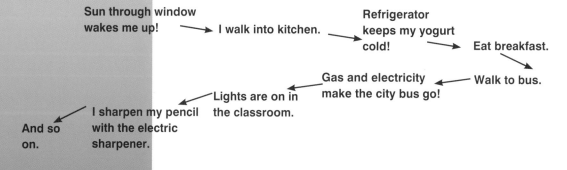

Sun through window wakes me up! → I walk into kitchen. → Refrigerator keeps my yogurt cold! → Eat breakfast. → Walk to bus. → Gas and electricity make the city bus go! → Lights are on in the classroom. → I sharpen my pencil with the electric sharpener. → And so on.

What Form Am I?

METHODS:

1. Ask the children to stand with you and shimmy and shake. Tell them that when you say, "Freeze!" they are to stop moving. When you say, "Wiggle!" they can move again. Play this game a few times.

2. Ask the children what they notice about their bodies when they freeze. What are they doing? What does it feel like when we freeze? How does it feel when we move?

3. Give the children small books, and show them how to balance the books on their heads. Can they do it? Do the books fall? Can they walk around the room—or even just take a couple of steps—with the books on their heads? Why is that so difficult? When they are moving, is the book moving, too? What makes the books go from resting on their heads to falling onto the floor?

4. Put the books aside, and transition into another activity. Gather the children into small groups, and give them dominoes or plank blocks. They will make a domino line to play with the idea of potential and kinetic energy. Show them how to stand the dominoes or planks on end and create a chain. When they are ready, let them tip the first domino, transferring energy from their hand into the domino, which should start a chain reaction. Let them explore making the dominoes topple over in a line.

5. While playing with the dominoes, introduce the terms *potential energy* and *kinetic energy*.

ESSENTIAL QUESTION:
How can we tell potential energy from kinetic energy?

OBJECTIVE:
▶ Children will explore forms of energy.

MATERIALS:
dominoes
thin plank blocks, such as Kapla blocks
small books, one for each child

ENERGY—Chapter Five

SCIENCE—Not Just for Scientists!

Potential Energy: the energy of position or rest

All objects sitting in place have potential energy.

Kinetic Energy: the energy of motion

Objects can transition from having potential energy to kinetic energy, but they need to be acted upon. They don't change states on their own!

6. Bring the discussion of potential energy and kinetic energy back to the books again. When the books are on your head and are resting, what kind of energy do they have? How about when the book is falling? What kind of energy does your body have when it is moving?

7. Play the energy dance game again, this time using the term *potential* instead of *freeze* and *kinetic* instead of *wiggle*.

Get Wired!

METHODS:

1. Turn the classroom lights on and off a few times. Ask the children what is happening. If you have other electricity-powered objects in the room, toggle them on and off, too. Do the same with toys or objects that run on batteries. Ask the children to offer their explanations for how that happens.

2. Put the children in small groups. Give each group a collection of electrical components. If you have enough for each to have a battery and a small fan or buzzer, that would be great!

3. Rather than giving the children the formula for building a circuit, let them try to get a small fan or buzzer to turn on. Give them time and space to explore. This may take a lot of discipline on your part to just let them play with and explore the components of the circuit, but the payoff will be worth it.

ESSENTIAL QUESTION:
How can we create a simple circuit?

OBJECTIVE:

▶ Children will play with electrical components to get a basic understanding of circuits.

Safety note: Do this activity with children who are no longer mouthing objects and who can carefully follow directions and safety instructions.

MATERIALS:
alligator clips
batteries
buzzers
small fans
wires

Where Can I Find the Materials?

Inexpensive solar panels, electrical components, and equipment are available online through retailers such as American Science and Surplus, www.sciplus.com, and Hand2Mind, www.hand2mind.com.

ENERGY—Chapter Five

69

4. If they need help, give them hints only. The most useful are that the electricity needs to travel through the wire and that wire has to touch metal.

5. If playing with the circuits makes you uneasy, or if the children need more guidance, provide them with a simple drawing of a circuit to guide their exploration. On a large paper or whiteboard, draw the diagram below:
Ideally, you can create an electricity station where the children can come and go and play around with circuits.

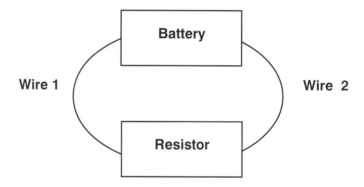

Here Comes the Sun

ESSENTIAL QUESTION:
How does the sun give us power?

OBJECTIVE:

▶ Children will use solar cells to explore an alternate form of energy.

MATERIALS:
lamp (to power solar cells) or sunlight
motor or fan
small solar panels (1.5V+)

METHODS:

1. Show children a large photo of the sun and elicit their knowledge of the sun. What is it? What do they know about how it works? What does it do for us? Listen to their ideas.
2. Show them a small solar panel, and ask what they think it is. Have a volunteer help you connect the panel to the motor or fan. What happens? Ask the children, "Why isn't it working?" Listen to their ideas.
3. Move the solar cell into a light source or direct sunlight. What happens? Where is the power coming from?
4. Give the children solar cells and motors or fans. Allow them time to build circuits with the solar cells and to test them with different amounts of sunlight or lamp light. They can try blocking the sun with their hands or a book to see what happens. Encourage them to explore in any way they would like.

What Is the Sun?

The sun is the closest star to Earth. It is the center of our solar system. At its core, it burns at 15 million degrees Celsius. The energy produced by the sun provides all of the heat and light we receive on Earth. For more interesting facts about the sun, see http://solarsystem.nasa.gov/planets/profile.cfm?Object=Sun.

Clay Play

ESSENTIAL QUESTION:

How do objects transform?

OBJECTIVES:

▸ Children use energy to change the shape of clay.

▸ Children learn that mass stays the same even if shape changes.

MATERIALS:

chart paper

marker

play clay or playdough

triple beam balance or scale

METHODS:

1. Give each child a piece of clay. Let him weigh his clay, and record the measurement on the paper.

2. Let each child play with the clay and mold it into any shape he likes.

3. As the children work, ask them to make observations about how working with the clay changes it. Encourage them to think about the temperature of their hands and how the clay moves. Is it easier to work the clay when it is warm?

4. After the children have worked the clay for a while, let them measure it again. Has the mass changed? Ask them to offer explanations for what they observe.

5. Ask the children to break their clay into two parts and make two objects. Have them determine the mass of both objects. What do they find? (Each child's two pieces can be put on the balance or scale at the same time.)

6. Continue the taking-apart idea: Have them make three, four, and five objects from the same clay they started with. Continue to measure the mass and record their observations.

7. When exploration is complete, have them combine their smaller objects back into one lump of clay. Is that the same clay they started with? What do they notice about it now? Take one last measurement if they are interested.

CHAPTER SIX

Systems

What makes a good problem solver? People who are good at solving problems are able to see how things are connected. Where one person might see a stand-alone issue or idea, others can see relationships. They see a system and know that if one part of the system is not working, then eventually the whole system could fail.

Being aware of and studying relationships are keys in science and scientific thinking. We engage children with these ideas because our universe and everything in it is connected and organized into systems. Thinking this way transforms our world from a collection of seemingly disparate elements to that of organized, interrelated phenomena.

What is a system? *The Framework for Science Education* defines a *system* as "an organized group of related objects or components that form a whole." With this definition in mind, it is easy to see how children interact with numerous systems on a daily basis. They ride a subway or travel on roads that connect different parts of their community. They eat, their food travels through their digestive systems, and eventually they poop! They attend school, which is made up of classrooms, staff, schedules, and rules. They go to the playground, an organized collection of climbing materials and play spaces that flow from one to another.

Given that our world is a collection of systems, we can help children understand them by exploring complete systems and their components. Children can learn important lessons about connections and relationships. We can help them think strategically and analytically, making them better problem solvers and critical thinkers. Systems thinking and the ability to see the big picture are important aspects of cultivating the scientific mind.

SCIENCE—Not Just for Scientists!

ESSENTIAL QUESTION:

How are water systems connected?

OBJECTIVE:

▶ Children will explore the interconnected nature of water.

MATERIALS:

marker

mason jar with lid

paper

photos of lakes, ponds, streams, rivers, swamps, clouds, and oceans

water source (sink)

Water, Water Everywhere

METHODS:

1. Ask the children to name all the types of bodies of water they can think of, such as ponds, lakes, streams, rivers, bogs, oceans, and so on. Some may know the actual names of specific bodies of water. Make a list, and add some of your own ideas to keep the sharing flowing.

2. Share photos of different bodies of water. Explore the similarities and differences of each of the items on the list and in the photos. Ask the children for their ideas about the sizes, kinds of water, what animals live there, what plants live there, and so on.

3. Ask them where the water in each of these places comes from. Does it travel? Where does it flow? Listen to their ideas.

4. As part of your discussion, make a very simple explanation of the water cycle: rain falls into streams, streams flow into rivers, rivers flow into oceans, clouds form over oceans, clouds drop rain.

5. Do a simple experiment to let them see evaporation, condensation, and precipitation: Fill a jar about one-third full with water and draw a line on the outside of the jar to mark the water "start" line. Cap the jar tightly, and put it in a sunny or warm spot or use a lamp to simulate the sun. Each day encourage the children to observe the jar and talk about what they see happening.

My Body

ESSENTIAL QUESTION:

What systems make up our bodies?

OBJECTIVE:

▶ Children will learn about the systems of their bodies to see how they work together and separately.

MATERIALS:

photos and charts of body systems, including skeletal, muscular, digestive, and circulatory

METHODS:

1. Show the children a photo of a human skeleton. Ask them what they see. What are these things? Where are they in our bodies? What else is part of our bodies? Listen to their ideas.

2. Explore each layer of the body. Start with skin. Have them touch their own arms—what is that covering? How much of our body does it cover?

3. Move on to the muscles, bones, and blood: What is underneath the skin? How do we move? How do our muscles move? How are they connected? Where are our bones? How do you think the bones and muscles work together? What would we look like without bones? Let the children examine photos of the muscles and bones and circulatory system.

4. What else is inside our bodies? See if they can name any organs, such as lungs, heart, stomach, intestines, bladder, and so on. Can they explain what any of these organs do? Let them examine the photos so they can see how the parts of a system are connected.

ESSENTIAL QUESTION:

How do we use transportation?

OBJECTIVES:

▶ Children will build understanding of the ways we transport ourselves.

▶ Children will create a map of connecting pathways for travel.

MATERIALS:

building toys, such as Legos, blocks, TinkerToys, and so on

crayons

large butcher paper

paper

pictures of cars, buses, trains, bicycles, and other transportation devices

playdough

markers

How Do We Get from Here to There?

METHODS:

1. Ask the children how they get around your community. Do they ride in a car or truck? Do they walk? Do they ride a bicycle or trike? Record their answers on paper. Ask what other forms of transportation people use every day. Add those answers to the list.

2. For each mode of travel, ask the children what path these vehicles travel on, such as train tracks, roads, bike lanes, rivers, and so on.

3. Let each child or pair of children choose a form of transportation. Encourage them to create a representation of that vehicle. They can draw or create out of blocks, TinkerToys, cardboard, clay, or any other medium you have handy.

4. Ask them to think about how that vehicle is powered: Does it have an engine? Does a person make it go? Does it use oars?

5. On one large piece of butcher paper, encourage each child or pair of children to draw the path for their vehicle. They can create large or small pathways. Their pathways can be rivers, roads, bike paths, sidewalks, or any path they think is appropriate. As they work, help them think about what paths would be near to each other. Would they connect, overlap, or intersect?

6. When they are satisfied with their paths, let them play with their models on the map they have created.

Exploring an Ecosystem

METHODS:

1. If there is a wooded area nearby, take a stroll with the children. As you walk, ask the children to observe their surroundings. What living things are part of the forest ecosystem? What do they see? What do they hear? How do they know what other critters live there?

ESSENTIAL QUESTION:

How can we model an ecosystem?

OBJECTIVES:

▶ Children will learn what an ecosystem is.
▶ Children will create a model of a local ecosystem.

MATERIALS:

Note: Your materials will vary depending on your local ecosystem. This example is written for a forest ecosystem.

camera (if possible)

containers for your ecosystem model, such as large jars, large soda bottles, or clear plastic boxes

items collected outdoors, such as leaves, sticks, twigs, soil, and so on

markers or crayons

paper

SYSTEMS—Chapter Six

77

2. Collect samples along the way, being careful to avoid poisonous or potentially harmful plants. Leave bugs and other creatures where you find them.

3. If you have a camera handy, take photos of insects, large plants, animals, birds, and anything else the children notice. Use these photos for display or as part of later exploration.

4. When you return from your walk, talk about what you have seen. Let the children share their observations, and create a list of all they noticed.

5. Discuss each item on the list. For example, if they noticed a bird, talk about where they saw it, what it was doing, what it might eat, and so on. When talking about a tree, discuss the tree's need for water, sunlight, and soil. Point out that the tree provides a home for animals (such as birds), shade, oxygen, and so on. Help the children see the connections so they recognize that the forest is really a system, an *ecosystem:* a community of plants, animals, and the environment where they live.

6. Provide the materials and give the children time to create a model of what they have seen on their walk. Talk about the parts of the ecosystem and how they might represent them in their models. If you took photos on your walk, the children may wish to incorporate them into their models.

I Love My Bicycle

ESSENTIAL QUESTION:
How do the parts of a bicycle work together?

OBJECTIVE:
▶ Children will examine the parts of a bicycle to determine how the connections between parts work.

METHODS:

1. If you can go outside and pedal a bicycle, that is a great kick off! Let the children observe an adult (who is wearing a helmet) peddling a bicycle. Ask them to notice how the peddler's legs are working, how the pedals move, how the tires move, what the chain does, and so on. If you cannot do a live demonstration, show a video of a bicycle rider. Ask the children to share their observations.

2. Show the children photos of bicycles, and help them name the parts of a bicycle.

MATERIALS:
gears (a toy version is great)
photos of bicycles
pulleys
small bicycle or toy model bicycle
string
video of bicycle riders
wheels

3. Ask them to point out which parts are connected to other parts. If you have a bicycle or model, rotate the pedals so the children can observe what happens. (This is best done by turning the bike upside down and resting it on the seat and handlebars.) Ask them to share their observations.

4. Based on their interest and questions, explore the connections between the pedals, the crank, the crankset, the chain, the cassette, and the wheel.

5. Give the children the gears, wheels, pulleys, and string to explore. If you have the materials, they can try to create their own model of the pedaling system using string and gears.

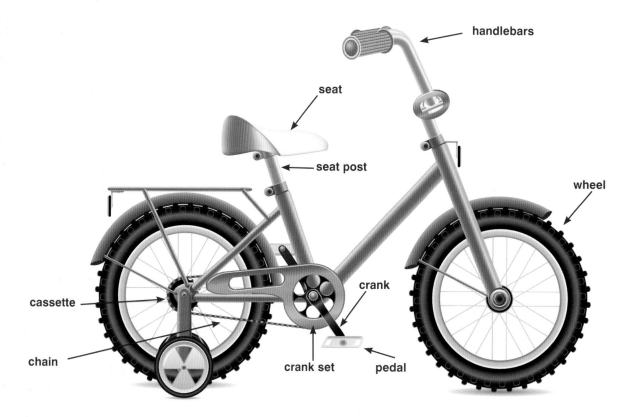

CHAPTER SEVEN

How Things Work

Children are curious about how things work. This interest ranges from their own bodies to a bicycle to the latest piece of technology they are playing with. We have all encountered the questions from young children: How are buildings built? How does a car work? Why does my heart beat? How does a flower grow?

Give your budding engineers and curious scientists opportunities to explore, look inside, design, build, and test objects they want to examine. You do not need to know exactly how the object you are exploring works. Sometimes it is better not to fully understand the mechanisms! Instead, focus on the inquiry and the exploration of the object. The process is key.

Give children opportunities to take items apart and ask questions about what they find. Then, allow them to use the parts to either reconstruct the items or to construct objects of their own creation. Both of these practices help children understand and develop the scientific, engineering mind-set of design, test, and refine.

There is a lot of power in helping children understand how things work and how things are made. Cultivate creative thinking as a way for children to make connections, see the intersection of how things work with how they are made, and learn how these items are used. As our world becomes more automated and the

focus on technology increases, it is helpful to go back to basics and help children understand how nonmotorized things work. From there they can begin to see how electricity and computer programming have helped us develop more and more complex tools and machines.

Each of the options in this chapter can be truly open ended. Do not fear that content is not being transmitted. Through their explorations of how things work, children are exposed to scientific and engineering thinking and will gather content along the way—content that they deeply understand because they are leading their own learning.

Take It Apart!

ESSENTIAL QUESTION:
How can we see how a machine works?

OBJECTIVE:

▸ Children will deconstruct the innards of a piece of equipment.

MATERIALS:

any old, broken or unused equipment, such as a computer, radio, cell phone, or electric toothbrush
large paper
marker
other tools as necessary
screwdrivers
small paper cups
wrenches

METHODS:

1. Place the equipment on a table. Ask the children to examine the object without touching it. What is it? What does it do? How does it work? Does it need electricity? Who made it? What materials is it made of? What is on the inside? Gather their answers. Record them if you like; otherwise, just have a discussion with their ideas.

2. Working with the children, identify different parts and talk about what they might do.

3. Using the proper tools, take the object apart. As you do so, point out each aspect and ask about its function. For example, if you are undoing a screw, ask the children what the function of the screw is and how it works. Dismantle the equipment to the level you are comfortable.

4. As you take the item apart, ask the children to sort the components in any way they choose. Talk with the children about how they are sorting the items—by color, shape, function, or some other criterion?

5. This activity will generate lots of questions. Record the children's questions on paper and use them for later explorations.

Build a Model

ESSENTIAL QUESTION:

How do we make a model of a familiar object?

OBJECTIVES:

▶ Children will examine the parts of a familiar object.

▶ Children will build a model out of toy parts or other reusable materials.

MATERIALS:

cardboard tubes and boxes

glue

photos or model of a mechanical object, such as a scooter, bicycle, crane, or truck

tape

TinkerToys or other building toys

METHODS:

Note: These steps describe the activity when using a scooter. Use any object you or the children select.

1. Examine the scooter. Ask who rides a scooter. Ask a volunteer to explain how he thinks the scooter works.

2. Review each part of the scooter. Look at the deck (where the foot goes), and ask what it is made of. What body part goes there? Move on to the wheels: What are they made of? How do they work? How do they spin? What is the brake used for? How do you use it? What is it made of? What are the handlebars made of? What are they shaped like? What are they used for?

3. Compare and contrast the different materials used to build the scooter. Talk about what parts move and what parts do not move.

4. Using the materials you have on hand, work with the children to build a model of the scooter.

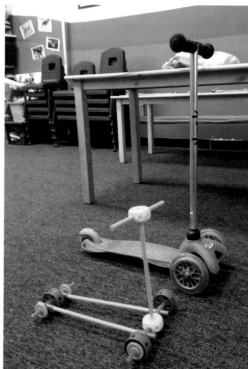

Simple Machines

ESSENTIAL QUESTION:
What are the first machines that did work?

OBJECTIVE:
▶ Children will explore the simple machines.

MATERIALS:
Note: There are simple machine kits on the market, or TinkerToys sets have many of these parts. You can also find them in common objects.
Examples of simple machines:
▶ inclined plane (board or thick piece of cardboard)
▶ lever (sturdy stick or metal rod)
▶ pully (wheel and string)
▶ screw
▶ wedge (wedge-shaped block)
▶ wheel and axle (real ones or toy version)
balls
blocks
cardboard tubes and boxes
straws

METHODS:

1. Place the simple machines on the floor or table. Give the children time to touch, examine, and play with each one.

2. As they explore, ask them what they think these items are. Have they seen them before? What are they used for? Gather as much information from the children as you can.

3. Let the children select a simple machine and play with it to figure out how it works. Provide them with additional building and exploration materials. Let the children explore uses for the machine.

4. In pairs or small groups, encourage the children to combine simple machines to create something. This could be as simple as having them build a car with a box, a wheel, and an axle. Or they might create a seesaw with the lever and wedge. The aim is for them to see how these objects work separately and together.

5. For children who need more of a challenge, ask them to make a contraption that solves a problem, such as one that lifts a block 10 centimeters in the air, moves a book 5 centimeters sideways on a table, or lifts an object that weighs 20 grams.

SCIENCE—Not Just for Scientists!

Tinker Time

ESSENTIAL QUESTION:
How can we design and build our own contraptions?

OBJECTIVE:
▶ Children will create and build a contraption or item of their own design.

MATERIALS:
balls
blocks
found objects (rocks, egg cartons, boxes, string, and so on)
funnels
masking tape
motors
planks
ramps
S hooks
simple machines
sticks
stiff cardboard
straws
If possible, a pegboard is useful. A carpeted or felt-covered wall can be used with Velcro to attach items as well.

METHODS:

1. Provide a variety of materials for the children to explore. Place boxes of objects around the room or on tables. Young children can work alone or with a partner, depending on their interest.
2. Help the children do an inventory of the materials. They can name things and speculate on what the items might be used for.
3. Give children their challenge: Create a contraption or a goofy machine that uses these items.
4. As they work, observe them and comment as appropriate: "Laura, I see you connected the wheel to a string. You created a pulley."

Suspension Bridge

METHODS:

1. Show the children photos of different suspension bridges, such as the Severn Bridge in Britain, the Golden Gate Bridge in San Francisco, or the Akashi Kaikyo Bridge in Japan. Discuss what they notice about each one. Create a list of features that the bridges have in common.

2. Divide the children into small groups, and give each group two lengths of rope, two chairs, and four pieces of tape. Give them time to try to create a model of a suspension bridge with these objects.

3. When they have finished, let them observe one another's work and ask for comments and questions. Ask them about their process and why they made the choices they did.

ESSENTIAL QUESTION:

How does a suspension bridge stand up?

OBJECTIVE:

▸ Children will explore the basic structure of a suspension bridge to determine what makes it stand up.

MATERIALS:

blocks
cardboard
chairs (enough for each group to have two)
equal lengths of rope (enough for each group to have two)
marker
masking tape
paper
photos of various suspension bridges
yarn

SCIENCE—Not Just for Scientists!

4. Ask them if any corrections need to be made. Encourage them to refine their designs.

5. If they would like to go deeper, give them building materials such as cardboard, blocks, paper, yarn, and tape, and encourage them to build smaller-scale models of a suspension bridge.

6. If they are interested, they can test the strength of their bridges by stacking pennies, blocks, or books. They can design, test, and redesign until they are satisfied with their creations.

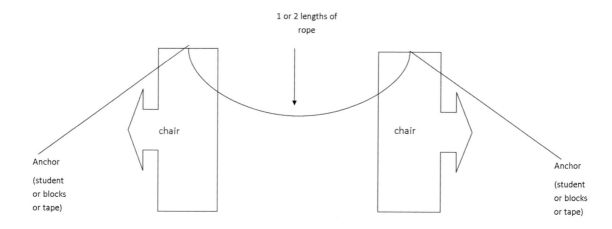

1 or 2 lengths of rope

chair   chair

Anchor   Anchor

(student   (student
or blocks   or blocks
or tape)   or tape)

Resources

MATERIALS

Collect found objects or items from your personal journeys: rocks, shells, feathers, leaves (that you can press and laminate), pinecones, paper towel tubes, plastic and paper containers, plastic carton tops, and so on. These will come in handy!

Additionally, following are some of my favorite science-supply vendors:

- American Science and Surplus: www.sciplus.com
- Bio Corporation: www.biologyproducts.com
- Carolina Biological Supply: www.carolina.com
- ETA Hand2Mind: www.hand2mind.com
- Storefront Science: www.storefrontscience.com—offers selected science, logic, and math games, toys, and materials

BOOKS FOR TEACHERS AND PARENTS

If you are interested in adding to your reference shelf and want to find more ideas to help children with their explorations, these books are nice to have. While some have activities, others explain content really well. Choose the ones that fill the holes in your knowledge. A membership in the National Science Teachers Association, or just a visit to their website (www.nsta.org), can provide you with many excellent ideas.

Ardley, Neil. 2006. *101 Great Science Experiments: A Step-by-Step Guide.* New York: DK Publishing.

Caduto, Michael J. 2011. *Catch the Wind, Harness the Sun: 22 Super-Charged Science Projects for Kids.* North Adams, MA: Storey Publishing.

Leslie, Clare Walker. 2010. *The Nature Connection: An Outdoor Workbook.* North Adams, MA: Storey Publishing.

Ottewell, Guy. 1989. *The Thousand-Yard Model or the Earth as a Peppercorn.* Raynham, MA: Universal Workshop.

Quinn, Helen, Heidi Schweingruber, and Thomas Keller, eds. 2012. *A Framework for K–12 Science Education: Practices, Crosscutting Concepts, and Core Ideas.* Washington, DC: The National Academies Press.

Russell, Helen Ross. 1998. *Ten-Minute Field Trips: A Teacher's Guide to Using the Schoolgrounds for Environmental Studies.* 3rd ed. Arlington, VA: NSTA Press.

Tierra, Lesley. 2000. *A Kids' Herb Book for Children of All Ages.* San Francisco: Robert Reed.

VanCleave, Janice. 1989. *Chemistry for Every Kid: 101 Easy Experiments that Really Work.* Hoboken, NJ: Jossey-Bass.

VanCleave, Janice. 1991. *Earth Science for Every Kid: 101 Easy Experiments that Really Work.* Hoboken, NJ: Wiley.

VanCleave, Janice. 1996. *Ecology for Every Kid: Easy Activities that Make Learning Science Fun.* Hoboken, NJ: Wiley.

VanCleave, Janice. 2005. *Energy for Every Kid: Easy Activities that Make Learning Science Fun.* Hoboken, NJ: Wiley.

BOOKS FOR CHILDREN

I encourage you to build a science library for children. That way, as they are exploring and generating questions, you will have resources for them to turn to. There are a lot of great books out there that cover the sciences, but sometimes they can be inaccurate, which is also a great teaching opportunity. Take your time to choose books wisely.

Usborne's Discovery series and Beginners series are great references for individual animals, groups of animals, and specific science concepts. Scholastic's Discover More series and the Magic School Bus series are perennial favorites. Specifically, I recommend the following:

Arlon, Penelope. 2012. *Planets.* New York: Scholastic.

Arlon, Penelope, and Tory Gordon-Harris. 2012. *See Me Grow.* New York: Scholastic.

Cassino, Mark. 2009. *The Story of Snow: The Science of Winter's Wonder.* San Francisco: Chronicle Books.

Daynes, Katie. 2009. *See Inside Space.* London: Usborne.

DK Publishing. 1997. *The Big Book of Animals.* London: Dorling Kindersley.

Frith, Alex. 2012. *See Inside Inventions.* London: Usborne.

Frith, Alex, and Colin King. 2007. *See Inside Science.* London: Usborne.

Gilpin, Rebecca, and Leonie Pratt. 2009. *Big Book of Science Things to Make and Do.* London: Usborne.

Katzen, Mollie, and Ann Henderson. 1994. *Pretend Soup and Other Real Recipes: A Cookbook for Preschoolers and Up.* Berkeley, CA: Tricycle Press.

Lacey, Minna. 2012. *Big Book of Big Sea Creatures.* London: Usborne.

Mason, Conrad. 2010. *See Inside How Things Work.* London: Usborne.

McNulty, Faith. 2005. *If You Decide to Go to the Moon.* New York: Scholastic.

Pinnington, Andrea. 2012. *My Body.* New York: Scholastic.

Smith, Alistair, ed. 1996. *Big Book of Experiments.* London: Usborne.

Weitekamp, Margaret. 2013. *Pluto Secrets: An Icy World's Tale of Discovery.* New York: Abrams.

APPS

Many children today have access to digital technology and play on smartphones, tablets, and computers. The following apps can come in handy as quick references.

▶ **3D Brain**
Cold Spring Harbor Laboratory
Lets users explore the structure and functions of the brain.

▶ **3D Heart**
Cold Spring Harbor Laboratory
Lets users explore the structure and functions of the heart.

▶ **BioIQ Biology Picture Game**
Clef Software, Inc.
A simple game that gives users the chance to practice labeling different parts of cells and other biological structures.

▶ **BrainPOP**
BrainPOP Education

A favorite with children of all ages. The facts, movies, and games have strong science content.

▶ **Color Uncovered**

Exploratorium

One of the best and coolest science apps out there! Interactive and informative with super design. For iPad only.

▶ **Leafsnap**

Columbia University, the University of Maryland, and the Smithsonian Institution

Identifying a tree just got easier! Snap a photo of a leaf, and receive accurate information on the species. Currently, the app is a field guide to trees found in the northeastern United States. Eventually, it will include trees from across North America.

▶ **Moon Globe**

Midnight Martian

Similar to Star Walk, this app gives you lots of information about the moon.

▶ **Science 360**

National Science Foundation

Great for research and reference, as it has numerous videos and great photos. For iPad only.

▶ **Science on the Go**

Storefront Science

This app is one of the few designed for children to direct their own learning. It allows children to explore a specific location, such as On the Beach, and invites them to conduct simple experiments, share their findings, and go deeper.

▶ **Sound Uncovered**

Exploratorium

Interactive and informative with super design. For iPad only.

▶ **Star Walk**

Vito Technology, Inc.

Point your device at the sky, day or night, and get information about stars, constellations, and planets.

▶ **Trees Pro HD**
Nature Mobile
A field guide to trees found in North America and Europe. The free version includes forty trees; the in-app purchase option includes more than 160 species.

WEBSITES

Thanks to search engines, it is easy today to find web-based resources. Here are few that are worth a visit:

www.brainpop.com
Like the app, but with more!

www.exploratorium.edu
Website for the Exploratorium, one of my favorite science spots in the world.

www.khanacademy.org
The how-to spot for learning. If you want to make sure you understand a science concept, watch one of these videos.

www.nsta.org
National Science Teachers Association

http://ocean.si.edu
The Smithsonian National Museum of Natural History

www.pbs.org
PBS has links to their science and children's programs, with additional content, activities, and games.

www.ssec.si.edu
The Smithsonian Science Education Center

www.youtube.com/user/minutephysics
Short, super videos about physics and other scientific phenomena.

Index

SCIENCE—Not Just for Scientists!

SCIENCE—Not Just for Scientists!